Elite, Nottingham (1921; architects: Adamson & Kinns). This city centre cinema is seen in later years before bingo and nightclub use.

Old Cinemas

Allen Eyles

A Shire book

CONTENTS

Cover: *Odeon, Harrogate (1936; architects: Harry Weedon, J. Cecil Clavering). This is one of the few original Odeons to retain its original name sign and continue operating successfully in 2001.*

ACKNOWLEDGEMENTS

All illustrations are from the author's collection (except Odeon South Harrow, courtesy of Derek Knights). Photographs of the Duke of York's Brighton, Electric Palace Harwich, Odeons at Harrogate, Marble Arch, Muswell Hill and Elephant and Castle are copyright © Allen Eyles. The photograph of the auditorium of the Electric Notting Hill is used by courtesy of the former GLC Department of Architecture and Civic Design; of the Elite Nottingham courtesy of the former EMI Cinemas; of Green's Playhouse Glasgow courtesy of the Scottish Film Archive; and of the Granada Bedford courtesy of Photo Coverage. All other photographs are believed to be out of copyright.

Special thanks to Jeffrey Richards for introducing author to publisher, and to John Fernee for reading the text.

British Library Cataloguing in Publication Data: Eyles, Allen. Old Cinemas. – (A Shire album; no. 357) 1. Motion picture theaters – Great Britain – History I. Title 725.8'23'0941. ISBN 0 7478 0488 5.

Published in 2001 by Shire Publications Ltd, Cromwell House, Church Street, Princes Risborough, Buckinghamshire HP27 9AA, UK. (Website: www.shirebooks.co.uk)
Copyright © 2001 by Allen Eyles. First published 2001. Shire Album 357. ISBN 0 7478 0488 5.
Allen Eyles is hereby identified as the author of this work in accordance with Section 77 of the Copyright, Designs and Patents Act 1988.

Printed in Great Britain by CIT Printing Services Ltd, Press Buildings, Merlins Bridge, Haverfordwest, Pembrokeshire SA61 1XF.

The Saturday morning Mickey Mouse Club at the Odeon, Kemp Town, Brighton, poses for a photograph.

INTRODUCTION

Film exhibition began as a novelty and became the pre-eminent form of mass entertainment for the first half of the twentieth century. Its evolution from fairground and music-hall attraction to a complete evening's sophisticated entertainment was accompanied by the rapid development of elaborate buildings designed to enhance the experience. The rise of television, video and increasing home comfort brought about predictions of the cinema building's demise and extinction. But film exhibition re-invented itself in the 1980s with the 'multiplex', which has spread world-wide, fuelling a huge recovery in attendances (albeit to a fraction of their earlier levels) but at the same time hurting, often fatally, the surviving cinemas of the pre-1939 'golden age'. This book charts the rise and fall in Britain of the traditional purpose-built single-screen cinema.

BEGINNINGS

Public film exhibition began in Britain on 21st February 1896 with a programme of shorts made by the Lumière brothers in Paris using their Cinématographe, shown in the Great Hall of the Polytechnic Institution in Upper Regent Street, central London. The Cinématographe was such a success that it transferred on 9th March to the Empire music hall in Leicester Square, where it ran for eighteen months as a twenty-minute star attraction on the bill. A rival British system, R. W. Paul's Theatrograph, was a public attraction at Olympia in March 1896 before being adopted by other theatres, and moving pictures were being presented across Britain by the end of the year. Fairground booths were also adapted to present films within months of the first show. Public halls were hired for nights of film shows by travelling showmen, while in July 1896 the short-lived conversion to a cinema of a shop in Fife Road, Kingston upon Thames, with brown paper over the windows and benches across the floor, was perhaps the first of many adaptations of shops, railway arches and halls into cinemas.

Although the Central Hall in Colne, Lancashire, opened in 1907, has been cited as an early purpose-built cinema, it seems to have been designed for many uses – it had a flat floor and numerous windows – and may have shown films only on two nights a week. A former swimming pool turned theatre at Balham, south London, switched to films only in about July 1907 and remained a cinema until 1960. The Gem, Great Yarmouth, was a spectacular cinema opened in July 1908 but it was originally conceived as a menagerie. By the following year, purpose-built cinemas began springing up throughout Britain and even small towns had full-time cinemas by the start of the First World War.

Queues at the Regent, Hanley (now a live theatre), for 'The Singing Fool', the first talking picture to be widely shown.

EARLY ELECTRIC PALACES

Some cinemas were individual local enterprises; others were part of small local chains or the first large circuits, such as those of Montagu Pyke and Biograph Theatres in the London area, Albany Ward in the west of England, New Century Pictures in the north, and BB Pictures in Scotland. The first national chain was that of Provincial Cinematograph Theatres (PCT), which established Picture Houses in large cities and was the only film exhibition company quoted on the Stock Exchange in 1913.

The cinemas of this period usually seated no more than 700 people on a single sloping floor under barrel-vaulted ceilings crossed by ribs of highly decorated plaster, with side-wall murals between pilasters. A small balcony was sometimes included. There was padded, tip-up seating in the better seats and rows of benches at the front, often reached by a separate side entrance. Exteriors were elaborate and eye-catching with paybox windows open to the street, although toilet facilities were minimal. A small stage was provided for live acts and announcements with an orchestra pit or similar enclosed space for musicians to accompany the silent films. The screen would be of solid white plaster, usually with rounded corners, set on the back wall and exposed to view rather than protected by curtains.

Some of the cinemas of this period have survived. The oldest one still operating without drastic modernisation is the Duke of York's at Brighton from 1910. The most complete example is the same year's Electric (also known as the Imperial Playhouse) at

Portobello Road, Notting Hill, London. Like other early halls, this started life as a lavishly appointed building showing the latest films but declined into a fleapit screening old releases after being superseded by larger newcomers. Most remarkably, it retains its ornamented picture-frame proscenium (whereas the Duke of York's was fitted with a new proscenium arch for wide-screen films in 1956). A restored London suburban example is the Brixton Electric Pavilion (1911), now the Ritzy. A rare small-town survivor is the Electric Palace (1911) at Harwich, Essex.

Above and right: *Duke of York's, Brighton (1910; architects: Clayton & Black). The oldest largely unaltered British cinema still operating has a can-can dancer's legs added to the frontage and a replacement proscenium arch inside.*

Above: *Electric, Portobello Road, Notting Hill (1910; architect: Gerald Seymour Valentin). This west London cinema is seen in c.1939 as a fleapit (exterior) and in 1972 (interior), with some renovation in progress (fully renovated since).*

Left: *Electric Pavilion, Brixton (1911; architects: Homes & Lucas). This single-floor cinema has now been restored as part of the Ritzy cinema complex in south London.*

Below: *Electric Palace, Harwich (1911; architect: Harold R. Hooper). 1983 views of this early, typical small-town cinema in Essex, which was restored by local initiative and has become a tourist attraction.*

Right and below: Carlton, Swansea (1914; architect: Charles Tamlin Ruthen). This city centre cinema was the last word in taste and refinement. Although the auditorium was demolished, its exterior has been restored and its foyer areas form part of a bookshop.

Much effort to create a luxurious and dignified atmosphere was made in city centres by PCT's Picture Houses and others to compete with live theatres and draw in the carriage trade at higher prices of admission. Here balconies were more common and the general decorative scheme often mimicked that of theatres and music halls. Almost all have disappeared through redevelopment. A rare and precious survivor is the West End, later the Rialto, in Coventry Street, close to Piccadilly Circus in London (although it has not been used as a cinema since 1982). The West End made a big impression on opening in 1913 through the first use of a neon sign in the centre of London, while its great arched window was outlined by white tubes filled with carbon dioxide gas. Pavilioned boxes were situated to each side of the balcony front. With its central dome and richly ornamented plasterwork finished in cream and gold, the West End had all the elegance of a live theatre. Its design included several floors of offices over the foyers and a large restaurant in the basement. Of equivalent city centre opulence was the Carlton, Swansea (1914).

After the arrival of longer 'feature-length' films around 1913, there was even more confidence in the future of the medium, and bigger cinemas began to appear, although the largest venues were usually

former music halls or converted skating rinks. One of the biggest developments was the 1914 Grange at Kilburn, north London, which seated over 2000 people and included a large café on the first floor. The architect was Edward A. Stone, one of several who specialised in cinema work.

By the end of 1914, there were some 440 cinemas in the London postal area and probably over 4000 across the whole of Britain. But many closed for good during the First World War when projectionists were drafted, films were in short supply, and an amusement tax from May 1916 took most from the cheaper tickets.

THE NINETEEN TWENTIES

After the war, an acute housing shortage led to a ban on 'luxury building' that lasted until 1921, when several large cinemas opened in major city centres, clearly influenced by and modelled on the unbridled expansion of movie theatres in North America. The first cinema to attract widespread respect in architectural circles was the Regent, Brighton, designed by Robert Atkinson and costing £400,000. The fan-shaped auditorium seated 2200 and a ballroom, which could accommodate 1700, was added above. Like virtually every large cinema of the 1920s, it had a restaurant as well (plus a café and tea room).

Then there were the Elite, Nottingham (1921), with the largest organ in a British cinema to that date, three cafés on different floors in Louis XVI, Jacobean and Dutch styles, and a meeting room in Georgian style; and the Capitol, Cardiff, seating 3000 and, apart from the roof, built entirely of reinforced concrete, with three restaurants, a banqueting suite, a basement ballroom and a small preview theatre.

In 1922 the large Piccadilly was built in Manchester, which, with its tall auditorium and two balconies, seemed more suited to live shows, while Leeds had its first large super cinema, the Majestic.

Although new suburban cinemas were generally more modest in size, in 1923 the Davis family were considered daring when they opened the Pavilion at Shepherd's Bush in west London, seating nearly 3000. Its architect, Frank T. Verity, was awarded a medal by the Royal Institute of British Architects for the exterior design.

Regent, Brighton (1921; architect: Robert Atkinson; interior decorations in collaboration with Walter Bayes). Exterior view dates from 1945, interior from 1920s. Note the deep stage, the orchestra in the pit to accompany the silent films, and the luxury settee seating in the front of the balcony. The richly decorated curved proscenium arch was destroyed in a fire in 1928 and replaced with a rectangular opening. Demolished in 1973.

8

Majestic, Leeds (1922; architects: P. J. Steinlet, J. C. Maxwell). This vast city centre cinema had a huge dome and a frieze of galloping horsemen.

Over the next two or three years few new cinemas opened. One cause of the lull was the increasing popularity of radio, which cut attendances. Then the big Hollywood companies began to build American-style movie palaces in Britain to launch their latest releases. In 1927 Paramount opened the Plaza at Piccadilly Circus in London's West End (and later built Paramount theatres in major city centres). The Plaza was followed in 1928 by Metro-Goldwyn-Mayer's new Empire on the site of the old music hall in Leicester Square, designed primarily by the Scots-born American architect Thomas W. Lamb. However, it was the Scottish Green family that in 1927 opened Green's Playhouse in the centre of Glasgow with the largest-capacity single-cinema auditorium ever created in Britain, crammed with 4346 seats on three levels at its peak in the Second World War. As at the Regent, Brighton, a huge dance hall was built over the theatre.

Pavilion, Shepherd's Bush (1923; architect: Frank T. Verity). This huge west London cinema lost its original auditorium to wartime bombing

Above: *Plaza, Piccadilly Circus (1926; architect: Frank T. Verity). The landmark exterior of this London West End cinema remains but the imposing American-style interior with two balconies (the lower one at street level) was replaced by smaller cinemas in 1967–8.*

Green's Playhouse, Glasgow (1927; architect: John Fairweather). The largest of all British cinemas in seating capacity has now been replaced by a multiplex.

Left and below: *New Victoria, Bradford (1930; architect: William Illingworth). The exterior of this enormous city centre cinema remains but the interior, subdivided for bingo and smaller modern cinemas, was disused in 2001.*

Expansion was in the air in 1927 with cinemas planned everywhere and mutterings of mysterious financial dealings. Fears of a full-scale invasion by American circuits proved unfounded as a new British concern, the Gaumont-British Picture Corporation, emerged. It was based on the existing Gaumont company but was an integrated combine that covered film production, distribution and exhibition. When Gaumont-British took over the huge PCT chain in 1929 it became a powerful force indeed. PCT's chief architect, W. E. Trent, completed many cinemas under construction, including the Regents at Hanley, Bournemouth and Ipswich and the New Victoria at Edinburgh (all 1929) while supervising others like the New Victoria, Bradford (also 1929). All these have survived, though often under different names and with extensive internal modernisation.

In 1928 Associated British Cinemas (ABC) was formed from three small existing circuits and linked to a major producer, British International Pictures, with studios at Elstree and a distribution set-up. ABC expanded rapidly by taking over and building cinemas to become the second combine that, with Gaumont, dominated the British film scene. Among its earliest purpose-built cinemas were the Regal, Glasgow (1929), and Savoy, Brighton (1930).

THE TALKIES

The arrival of sound films spurred new enthusiasm for the cinema although some patrons, mostly elderly, still preferred the music-inspired reverie of the 'silents' to the raucous and distracting combination of pre-recorded talk, sound effects and music (for which poor amplification systems and acoustics were often to blame). New screens had to be erected in existing cinemas with speakers behind.

Inspired by foreign examples, British cinemas became more adventurous and distinctive in their design. In the United States the architect John Eberson had pioneered the idea of the 'atmospheric' auditorium, which gave audiences the impression of sitting outdoors in an exotic, foreign setting. A vast, plain, curving ceiling was painted to represent the sky with twinkling lights for stars while projectors added moving cloud patterns. The lighting could be slowly changed to give a vivid impression of sunrise or sunset. The side walls resembled giant stage sets of foreign villages and castles with trees and bushes, while lanterns glowed dimly through the windows of the buildings, with eaves and roofs projecting into the auditorium. The proscenium arch often became a bridge that continued the theme and could be used by

Above and left: *Astoria, Brixton (1929; architect: E. A. Stone; decoration: Marc Henri). This atmospheric south London cinema opened with the talkies and variety shows and has survived as the Academy concert venue.*

12

Astoria, Finsbury Park (1930; architect: E. A. Stone; decoration: Marc Henri & Laverdet). A Moorish city lines the side walls of this north London cinema, restored for religious use.

live performers in the stage shows that frequently accompanied the films.

The most spectacular atmospheric cinemas in Britain were the Astorias at Brixton and Finsbury Park. Opened in 1929, the Brixton Astoria in south London offered an 'outdoor' setting of an Italian garden with colonnades flanking the proscenium adapted from Italian palaces. At Finsbury Park in north London (1930) the audience was surrounded by a Moorish walled city, with the proscenium arch representing a gateway. These vast auditoria made a strong impression on audiences often seeking refuge from cold, cramped dwellings.

Atmospheric schemes were successfully applied to new medium-sized cinemas: in

Avenue, Ealing (Northfields) (1932; architect: Cecil Masey). This atmospheric west London cinema, for most of its life an Odeon, is well preserved as a church.

13

New Victoria, Victoria (1930; architects: W. E. Trent, E. Wamsley Lewis). Now the Apollo Victoria live theatre, its auditorium has long been half-hidden behind the paraphernalia of the long-running musical 'Starlight Express'.

1930 at the Richmond (now the Odeon) at Richmond, Surrey, architects Leathart & Granger provided an auditorium that suggested the courtyard of a seventeenth-century Spanish grandee's house. The Avenue at Ealing, west London, displayed a courtyard in Spanish America; the buildings were decorated for a festive celebration while the 'sky' was hidden from view by tent-like drapes that offered protection from the blazing sun.

More daring and original was the concept behind the New Victoria at Victoria in central London (1930). A young architect, E. Wamsley Lewis, influenced by auditoria he had seen in Berlin (especially Hans Poelzig's Grosses Schauspielhaus), devised an underwater setting or 'mermaid's palace' with various marine motifs. The cinema had two matching exteriors on two streets in a severely modern style with pronounced horizontal banding that originally carried neon lighting contrasting with vertical columns over the entrances.

The New Victoria failed to impress one young cinema entrepreneur, Sidney Bernstein, who was starting to build

An organ interlude c.1930 at the Regent, Bristol, destroyed by wartime bombing.

14

Granada, Tooting (1931; architect: Cecil Masey; interior designer: Theodore Komisarjevsky). Opening views of foyer and auditorium, now pressed to bingo use and the first cinema building listed Grade I.

Granada cinemas. He thought that audiences preferred traditional design as opposed to anything provocatively new (in fact, most cinema-goers went for the films and accepted whatever cinema they were showing in as long as it was well run with good sightlines). In 1931 Bernstein opened, in the south London suburb of Tooting, the most spectacular of all the Granadas. The architect was Cecil Masey but the look of the foyer and vast auditorium (with 3086 seats) was the work of a Russian-born theatre designer and producer, Theodore Komisarjevksy. The foyer resembled a huge baronial banqueting hall with minstrels' gallery (which housed the cinema café) while the auditorium had a cathedral-like appearance with huge Gothic arches on the splay walls and a curious nod to the atmospheric style in the sections of ceiling painted to look like sky.

The Granada, Tooting, followed the Granada at Walthamstow, east London (1930), where Masey provided a Spanish-looking exterior and Komisarjevsky decorated the auditorium in Moorish style. After Tooting, in 1934, came the Granada at Maidstone, Kent, where Komisarjevsky designed a more economical but still opulent interior in Italian Renaissance style with richly decorated grille-work on the side walls and a huge chandelier suspended from the centre of a large roundel on the flat ceiling. This

interior scheme set the pattern with minor variations for several Granadas including Shrewsbury (1934), Bedford (1934), Harrow (1937) and Kingston (1939). Some important Granadas were given a more lavish treatment: Manchester (1935, sold to the rival Gaumont chain before opening), Clapham Junction in south London (1937), and, in the cathedral-like style of

Granada, Bedford (1934; architects: Benslyn, Morrison & Jordan; interior designer: Theodore Komisarjevsky). A lost example of the widespread 'standard' Granada style.

Gaumont Palace, Salisbury (1931; architect: W. E. Trent). This delightful Tudor scheme survives in sections following subdivision into a five-screen Odeon.

Tooting, Woolwich (1937). All the Granada cinemas featured cafés and virtually all had organs, which were a prominent part of the programme. Stage facilities were provided and often used for live acts (such as amateur talent contests) accompanying the films.

A few 1930s cinemas were skilfully decorated in the Tudor style, most notably the Beaufort at Ward End, Birmingham (1929), and the Gaumont Palace at Salisbury (1931), which used the existing historic Ye Halle of John Halle as its entrance and daringly but successfully adopted its style for the inner foyers and auditorium.

Another decorative method, promoted in the 1930s by the Holophane company and developed by Rollo Gillespie Williams, was the use of colour-changing lighting effects. At the Capitol, Didsbury, Manchester (1931), the rough-cast walls were treated with a white plastic paint on which, it was claimed, 5044 different lighting combinations could be played. Even the seats were specially treated to respond to the colours. The Capitol, Aberdeen (1933), had reflective silver paint on its grille-work. At the Palace, Conwy, in north Wales, one of many notable cinemas designed by Sidney Colwyn Foulkes, the screen was flanked on each side by six silvered columns that reflected colours and also bathed an intervening alcove in contrasting colours.

Palace, Conwy (1936; architect: Sidney Colwyn Foulkes). This luxurious north Wales cinema was designed for colour-changing lighting effects, which are not part of its current life as a bingo hall.

THE MODERN STYLE

By 1934 cinema design had come under the influence of the Modern Movement and presented a modern and forward-looking image. At the Dreamland, Margate, architects Leathart & Granger introduced the sleek fin tower that became a popular feature in front elevations.

It was the late-blooming Odeon chain that came to symbolise British cinema design at its more progressive and streamlined stage. The head of the circuit, Oscar Deutsch, began with modest cinemas in the Midlands and along the South Coast. His cinema at Perry Barr, Birmingham – a one-off venture in 1930 – was the first to use the Odeon name in Britain and the first to display the distinctive style of lettering, created by the sign manufacturer Harold Pearce, that became one of the most celebrated and widely recognised logos of any British company.

Deutsch's early Odeon at South Harrow, designed by local architect A. P. Starkey, was a low-cost building. It had a striking wide frontage clad in cream-coloured faience tiling with a deep central recess and a virtual absence of windows, plus two wings of shops and flats. This streamlined use of light-coloured faience, later relieved by thin colour bands, established a basic element of the Odeon style. The Odeon at

Dreamland, Margate (1935; architects: Leathart & Granger). This delightfully named seafront leisure complex had the earliest example of the fin tower. The cinema is now principally used for bingo.

Odeon, South Harrow (1933; architect: A. P. Starkey). This aggressively modern cinema (seen in 1949) in a west London suburb played a key role in establishing the Odeon circuit style but has now made way for flats.

Worthing (1934), from architects Whinney, Son & Austen Hall, contrasted faience with brick and added a striking vertical tower feature. The Nottingham architect T. Cecil Howitt refined the tower feature at the Warley Cinema (1934, soon renamed Odeon, Warley) with a broad, flat top supported by thick circular piers and added a basketweave pattern to the arrangement of faience tiles covering the entire frontage.

But it was the Birmingham practice of Harry Weedon, and in particular the genius of one assistant, J. Cecil Clavering, that gave the Odeon circuit its finest exteriors. For the Odeon (1935) at Kingstanding, a suburb of Birmingham, Clavering devised a

Odeon, Worthing (1934; architects: Whinney, Son & Austen Hall). The most spectacular of the early Odeons with rounded corner and tower, now demolished.

18

Odeon, Kingstanding (1935; architects: Harry Weedon, J. Cecil Clavering). The Odeon circuit style at its most assured, facing a roundabout in suburban Birmingham. The building is now a bingo club.

streamlined frontage with a subtle interplay of brick and faience and three central vertical fins (inspired, as Clavering has noted, by the Dreamland, Margate). For the Odeon at Sutton Coldfield (1936), Clavering came up with a similarly striking scheme for a corner entrance with the slab tower in cream faience enclosed by brickwork. These towers served to advertise the building for miles around with the word CINEMA lit up in neon. Neon tubing was also used to outline the shape of Odeons at night, and most 1930s cinemas made some use of neon and floodlighting to advertise their presence.

Odeon, Sutton Coldfield (1936; architects: Harry Weedon, J. Cecil Clavering). The perfected Odeon style with corner entrance. The building is still in use as a cinema, subdivided.

Left and below: *Odeon, Muswell Hill (1936; architect: George Coles). This Odeon makes typical use of faience in what was an aggressively modern exterior, especially for a sedate north London suburb. It has the best surviving Odeon interior with its striking central lighting strip plunging down towards the proscenium.*

Despite the early departure of J. Cecil Clavering, the Harry Weedon practice continued to design an amazing series of sleek, eye-catching Odeons, although in historic Chester (1936) and York (1937) the local authorities demanded less brash exteriors solely in brick with more traditional signage.

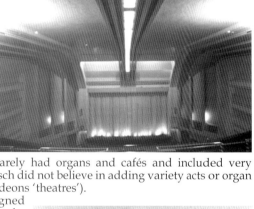

Inside, the Weedon Odeons had streamlined auditoria with stepped-down ceilings and usually modest decoration. They rarely had organs and cafés and included very limited stage facilities as Oscar Deutsch did not believe in adding variety acts or organ interludes (although he called his Odeons 'theatres').

Other architects also designed Odeons, adopting the house style. George Coles designed many fine cinemas: his Odeons at Acton, west London (1937), Balham, south London (1938), and Erith, Kent (1938), for example, had powerful exteriors entirely clad in cream-coloured faience. His interiors were often livelier than those of Weedon – most notably at Muswell Hill, north London (1936), with its Art Deco foyers and auditorium, the latter dominated by a linear light feature extending across the ceiling to plunge down towards the screen. Andrew Mather's practice also handled many new Odeons and some of these – mostly the work of his assistant Keith P. Roberts – exhibited considerable flair, including the Odeon at Camberwell, south London

Odeon, Camberwell (1939; architect: Keith P. Roberts for Andrew Mather). One of two mirror-image façades of this vast cinema at a major road junction in south London, closed in 1975 and since replaced by flats.

Left and below: *Odeon, Leicester Square (1937; architects: Harry Weedon, Andrew Mather). Still the flagship of the Odeon circuit in the centre of London's West End. Exterior largely intact, brilliantly outlined in blue neon at night, and interior partially restored after ruinous 1966 modernisation, with its Compton organ retained throughout.*

(1939), with its twin towers, use of vitrolite panels in place of faience, and remarkably simple auditorium.

When Oscar Deutsch had the old Alhambra Theatre in Leicester Square demolished to make room for his London flagship in 1937, the Weedon and Mather practices combined to devise an Odeon with a black frontage and huge tower. The auditorium was unusually intricate in treatment, with cove lighting across the ceiling that faded in sequence towards or away from the screen and sculptures of flying female figures on the splay walls. Most memorable were the seats, upholstered in imitation leopard skin.

After opening 136 new cinemas and acquiring almost as many existing ones, Deutsch's Odeon chain became a national rival to the older ABC and Gaumont circuits; each had its own exclusive weekly double-bill programme of new films.

The Odeon style influenced other architects and entrepreneurs, resulting in cinema exteriors of some considerable panache, as at the Regal, Boston (1937), Empire, Loughborough (1938 remodelling), Ritz, Ilkeston (1938), and Plaza, Port Talbot (1940), all of which had striking moderne interiors as well.

Under W. R. Glen, its chief architect, the ABC circuit opened ninety-eight new cinemas – mostly named Regal, Rex, Savoy or Forum – and developed a distinctive

Above and below: *Regal (ABC), Streatham (1938; architect: W. R. Glen). This south London ABC cinema had a spacious foyer and an auditorium with sharply etched ceiling and prominent grille-work characteristic of circuit architect Glen's work. The elegant foyer remained but the auditorium disappeared in subdivision. Closed in December 2000.*

image, perhaps most clearly expressed in the numerous lofty entrance halls with side staircases to the balcony, and in the heavily scalloped ceilings and prominent decorative grille-work of many auditoria. The former Regal at Halifax and the Savoy, Northampton, are among the few to survive without completely ruinous alteration.

At Gaumont-British, fifty-one new cinemas were opened in the 1930s including a huge Gaumont Palace at Hammersmith (1932), a scheme taken over from another company, and another at Taunton (1932), a palatial county-town venture designed by William T. Benslyn. Gaumont's chief architect, W. E. Trent, designed or collaborated on many accomplished Gaumonts, including: Lewisham, south London (1932), the perfect fan-shaped auditorium; Wood Green, north London (1934), with its globe light fittings and curved proscenium arch; and Bromley, Kent (1936), with its faience corner tower and astounding shell-like interior.

Left and below: *Gaumont Palace, Wood Green (1934; architects: W. E. Trent, Ernest Tulley). This large north London cinema, disused after years as a bingo hall, had an enticingly modern entrance hall and a striking curved proscenium arch imitating that of a landmark Berlin picture house.*

Gaumont, Bromley (1936; architect: W. E. Trent). This amazing interior survived until closure in 1961 and subsequent conversion into a department store.

Apollo, Ardwick (1938; architects: Peter Cummings, Alex M. Irvine, R. Gillespie Williams). This large Manchester cinema with a ceiling specially designed to reflect coloured light has become a live venue with very occasional Asian film shows.

Holophane devised a new idea of covering the front ceiling and side walls in small concave silvered circles to reflect coloured light projected from different angles and this was used to impressive effect at such cinemas as the Odeon, Yeovil (1937), and Apollo, Ardwick, Manchester (1938).

Interior designers such as John Alexander and the partnership of Eugene Mollo and Michael Egan made notable contributions to many cinemas. Alexander contributed the over-life-size mythical figures, horses and chariots flanking the proscenium arch at the Northwick, Worcester (1938). Mollo & Egan designed streamlined interiors, making much use of jazzy carpet patterns and ribbed plasterwork on the side walls and ceiling at the Regal, Wimbledon (1933), Ritz, Chelmsford (1935), Regal, Godalming (1935), and elsewhere, as well as the striking front-lit grille-work on the side walls of the Embassy cinemas at Esher and Chesham (both 1937).

While Odeons and other cinemas provided some of the most modern and daring architecture of the 1930s, some

Above: *Northwick, Worcester (1938; architect: C. Edmund Wilford). The imposing figures by interior designer John Alexander survive but this outlying former cinema has had problems finding a new use after years as a bingo hall.*

Right: *Embassy, Esher (1937; architect: David E. Nye). The striking front-lit side-wall panels by designers Mollo & Egan still delight cinema-goers but the painted foliage on the side walls of the balcony was long ago wiped out.*

Gaumont State, Kilburn (1937; architect: George Coles). The largest of English cinemas, in north London, had a skyscraper frontage and a neo-classical style interior, now enjoyed by bingo-players. The organ console (just visible at the edge of the proscenium arch) has been relocated to the main floor and is still played on occasion.

independent entrepreneurs preferred the neo-classical style to impress audiences and perhaps put them on their best behaviour. In Scotland, the Greens built huge Playhouses at Dundee (1936) and Wishaw (1940) with auditoria in theatrical style by John Fairweather (like his earlier Green's Playhouse in Glasgow). The Playhouse, Dundee (1936), did have an ultra-modern exterior with a tower feature designed by Joseph Emberton. Similarly, the largest cinema built in England – the Gaumont State at Kilburn, north London (1937), with 4004 seats, designed by George Coles for the Hyams brothers (in a partnership with Gaumont) – contrasted a modern exterior with a neo-classical interior. The outside was dominated by a huge tower resembling a New York skyscraper but the foyer had fake marble Corinthian columns and an elaborate chandelier copied from Buckingham Palace. The vast auditorium in French Renaissance style, although awe-inspiring, lacked the density of detail that Coles brought to an earlier Hyams project, the Trocadero at Elephant and Castle in south London (1930).

At the other extreme in size were some of the newsreel theatres that were often total reconstructions of early cinemas, or new buildings squeezed into tight and awkward sites. These usually seated no more than 300 and were extremely modern and streamlined in style. Robert Atkinson (with A. F. B. Anderson) designed an Art Deco gem in the News Theatre at Piccadilly Circus, London, while Alister G. MacDonald placed newsreel theatres above concourse level on stilts at London's Victoria and Waterloo stations in 1933 and 1934 respectively, and Cecil Masey designed the

25

Waterloo Station News Theatre (1934; architect: Alister G. MacDonald). Built over a side road with the entrance at one end of the concourse, this 248-seat cinema closed on feature films in 1970 and has been demolished.

Left and below: *Curzon, Mayfair (1934; architect: Francis Lorne). This purpose-built London art house was a model of simplicity, closed in 1963 for a replacement of some quality.*

underground News Theatre next to Leeds central station (1938).

Much skilful design went into the handful of purpose-built art houses, including the original Curzon, Mayfair (1934), and the Cosmo, Glasgow (1939), because audiences would expect and appreciate fine surroundings, while the Classic, Baker Street, London (1937), was a rare example of a cinema constructed to revive old films (there was a Classic circuit of older cinemas).

Even before the Second World War put a stop to new cinema construction, the rate of expansion had slowed down and some older cinemas, particularly in city centres (as in the case of the Piccadilly in Manchester), had been purchased by major retail stores to enable them to expand. The total number of operating cinemas in Britain reached a peak of 4901 in 1939.

Odeon, Marble Arch (1967; architect: T. P. Bennett & Son). This spacious auditorium with its giant screen has been lost to subdivision.

THE SECOND WORLD WAR AND AFTER

During the Second World War British cinemas offered a relatively safe haven from air raids and were one of the few sources of entertainment, although direct hits resulted in casualties and some sites were damaged beyond repair. Immediately after the war, the nation in celebratory mood pushed British cinema admissions to a record level of 1635 million in one year.

When television and increasing domestic comfort began eating into attendance figures, more films began to be made in colour, and CinemaScope (with stereophonic sound) was introduced in 1953, requiring many cinemas to widen their proscenium openings or erect new screens in front. The number of cinemas began to decrease, partly as a result of an insufficient supply of Hollywood films, and the sharpest decline took place shortly after the arrival of Independent Television (ITV) – admissions nearly halved between 1957 and 1960.

A few cinemas opened – in new towns (Hemel Hempstead, Harlow, Basildon) or as smaller replacements for older properties. The Empire, Leicester Square, retained its 1928 frontage but from 1962 the stalls area became a dance hall while the old balcony was transformed into a strikingly luxurious modern cinema, the swansong of architect George Coles, with dramatic use of concealed lighting and rocking seats. The basement Odeon, Haymarket (1962), with its walls of Thai silk and ceiling of open circles, was pleasing, while the Odeon, Marble Arch (1967), had a deep-curved screen, the largest in Britain. But the two outstanding new

Odeon, Elephant and Castle (1966; architect: Erno Goldfinger). This uncompromising replacement for a much larger cinema survives only in photographs and memory.

cinemas of the period were the replacement Curzon, Mayfair (1966), with its cavern-like auditorium, and the Odeon, Elephant and Castle (1966), replacing the much larger Trocadero, in which architect Erno Goldfinger provided a spartan building stripped of all inessentials.

SUBDIVIDE TO SURVIVE

Many still popular cinemas, like the Odeon, Leicester Square, and the Egyptian-styled Astoria, Streatham, south London, were deemed hopelessly old-fashioned in the Swinging Sixties and ruthlessly modernised. But other cinemas, particularly in poorer districts, were sold off for redevelopment or converted to different leisure uses: bowling alleys largely failed but bingo proved to have enduring popularity. As films began to play for extended periods at local cinemas, there was no real need for the larger auditoria to pack audiences in during a single week and so almost every profitable cinema was subdivided. At many Odeons and Gaumonts this took the economical form of dropping a wall to enclose two new mini-cinemas under the balcony while the rest of the auditorium functioned as the main cinema. Most of these conversions were unsatisfactory in terms of sightlines and ambience, and they damaged the reputation of cinemas as much as the excessive prices that came to be charged.

In 1985 the introduction of the American-style multiplex with the ten-screen cinema at the Point, Milton Keynes, was immediately successful, especially with young cinema-goers, leading to a new wave of cinema-building that killed off many older picture houses. Unfortunately, the major multiplex operators (mostly American) have played safe and their buildings have been depressingly dreary and unadventurous, lagging behind developments in architectural design.

Cinema-going itself has changed dramatically. In its heyday, there were often queues for seats, first outside, then in the inner foyer, then at the back or sides of the auditorium. Prices were stratified, with the best seats in the house, in the front circle, costing four times as much as those in the front stalls. Performances used to be continuous; typically a show lasted three hours or more with main feature, supporting feature, newsreel, trailers and advertisements, plus intervals for spotlighted girls to sell ice-creams and soft drinks from trays (some cinemas offered organ interludes and amateur talent contests). Smoking was rife. Programmes would run six days (down to two or three days with midweek changes) outside major city centres, with revival double-bills shown on Sundays (when most cinemas were not permitted to start until 4.30 p.m.).

If the atmosphere has changed, at least it has been possible to preserve some of the buildings. The first cinemas were listed Grade II by English Heritage in 1972: the Granada, Tooting, and New Victoria, London. Both would almost certainly have been demolished otherwise and have since prospered in new uses, as bingo hall and live theatre respectively. Further cinemas continued to be listed, reaching a total of 130. Then a generic survey of English cinemas was made, as a result of which thirty additional buildings were listed (of which only six were still showing films) and eight of those previously listed were upgraded (two still functioning as cinemas). The Granada, Tooting, became the first Grade I picture palace. But the sad truth is that recognition of the achievements of British cinema architecture has come after far too many notable cinemas have been demolished or badly altered, and even listing has not prevented further highly damaging but supposedly reversible alterations. It is mainly the owners and operators of the smaller, early cinemas who take pride in maintaining their buildings that enable present-day cinema-goers to see films in historically intact or restored surroundings at such places as the Duke of York's, Brighton, the Ritzy (ex Pavilion), Brixton, and the Electric Palace, Harwich.

FURTHER READING

Atwell, David. *Cathedrals of the Movies: A History of British Cinemas and Their Audiences*. Architectural Press, 1980.
Eyles, Allen. *ABC: The First Name in Entertainment*. Cinema Theatre Association/BFI Publishing, 1993.
Eyles, Allen. *Gaumont British Cinemas*. Cinema Theatre Association/BFI Publishing, 1996.
Eyles, Allen. *The Granada Theatres*. Cinema Theatre Association/BFI Publishing, 1998.
Gray, Richard. *Cinemas in Britain: One Hundred Years of Cinema Architecture*. Lund Humphries, 1996.
Richards, Jeffrey. *The Age of the Dream Palace*. Routledge & Kegan Paul, 1984.
Sharp, Dennis. *The Picture Palace and Other Buildings for the Movies*. Hugh Evelyn, 1969.

Picture House, the annual magazine of the Cinema Theatre Association, is a rich source of cinema history. (CTA Publications Officer, 34 Pelham Road, London N22 6LN.)

PLACES TO VISIT

OPERATING CINEMAS

When this book was completed (March 2001), the following buildings were the best of those old cinemas still showing films and preserving some of the atmosphere of the traditional cinema-going experience. (Parts of some of these cinemas are of no historic interest, having been modernised. The information in brackets after some of the cinemas listed refers to such areas.)

CHESHIRE
Odeon, Northgate Street, Chester CH1 2HO. Telephone: 0870 505 0007. (Exterior only.)
Plaza, Mersey Square, Stockport SK1 1SP. Telephone: 0161 477 7779 (box office). (Theatre and cinema.)

DERBYSHIRE
Scala, Market Place, Ilkeston DE7 5QB. Telephone: 0115 932 4612.

DORSET
Regent, Broad Street, Lyme Regis DT7 3TP. Telephone: 01297 442053.
Tivoli Theatre, 19–23 West Borough, Wimborne BH21 1LT. Telephone: 01202 848014 (box office). (Arts centre.)

ESSEX
Electric Palace, King's Quay Street, Harwich CO12 3ER. Telephone: 01255 553333.

KENT
Empire, Delf Street, Sandwich CT13 9HB. Telephone: 01304 620480 (infoline). (Not former stalls area.)
New Royal [Odeon], Market Place, Faversham ME10 7AG. Telephone: 01795 591211 (infoline).

LINCOLNSHIRE
Kinema in the Woods, Coronation Road, Woodhall Spa LN10 6QD. Telephone: 01526 352166. (Old cinema in former cricket pavilion.)

LONDON
Curzon, Curzon Street, Mayfair, W1 7AF. Telephone: 0871 871 0011.
Electric, Portobello Road, W11. Telephone: 020 7727 9958 (infoline).
EMD [Granada], Hoe Street, Walthamstow, E17. Telephone: 020 8520 7092. (Not downstairs small cinemas.)
Empire, Leicester Square, WC2H 7BA. Telephone: 0870 010 2030. (Not Empire 2 or 3.)
Gate, Notting Hill Gate, W11 3JZ. Telephone: 020 7727 4043 (infoline).
National Film Theatre, South Bank, SE1 8XT. Telephone: 020 7633 0274 (infoline). (NFT1 only.)
Odeon, Haymarket, SW1Y 4SD. Telephone: 0870 505 0007.
Odeon [Gaumont], Holloway Road, N7 6LJ. Telephone: 0870 505 0007. (Exterior and foyer only.)
Odeon, Leicester Square, WC2H 7LQ. Telephone: 0870 505 0007. (Not foyers.)
Odeon, Fortis Green Road, Muswell Hill, N10 3HP. Telephone: 0870 505 0007. (Not small lower cinemas.)
Phoenix [Rex], High Road, North Finchley, N2. Telephone: 020 8444 6789 (infoline).
Rio [Classic], Kingsland High Street, Dalston, E8 2BP. Telephone: 020 7241 9410 (infoline).
Ritzy [Pavilion], Brixton Oval, SW2. Telephone: 020 7733 2229 (infoline). (Not new additional cinemas.)
UGC [Carlton], Haymarket, SW1Y 4RQ. Telephone: 0870 907 0712. (Not downstairs cinemas.)

NORFOLK
Majestic, Tower Street, King's Lynn PE30 1EJ. Telephone: 01553 772603. (Not smaller cinemas.)

SOMERSET
ABC [Beau Nash], Westgate Street, Bath BA1 1EP. Telephone: 01225 461730.
Curzon, Old Church Road, Clevedon BS21 6NN. Telephone: 01275 871000 (infoline).
Odeon, The Centre, Weston-super-Mare BS23 1UR. Telephone: 0870 505 0007. (Exterior, foyers, cinema in former front stalls area only.)

SURREY
ABC [Embassy], High Street, Esher KT10 9RT. Telephone: 01372 465639. (Large auditorium only.)
Odeon [Richmond], Hill Street, Richmond TW9 1TW. Telephone: 0870 505 0007. (Not small lower cinemas.)

SUSSEX
Dome, Marine Parade, Worthing BN11 3PT. Telephone: 01903 200461.
Duke of York's Premier Picture House, Preston Circus, Brighton. Telephone: 01273 626261 (infoline).
Pavilion, George Street, Hailsham BN27 1AE. Telephone: 01323 841414.
Picturedrome, Canada Grove, Bognor Regis PO21 2AB. Telephone: 01243 841015. (Not small upstairs auditorium.)

WEST MIDLANDS
Odeon, Birmingham Road, Sutton Coldfield B72 1QL. Telephone: 0870 505 0007. (Exterior only. Auditorium lost through subdivision.)

WILTSHIRE
Odeon [Gaumont Palace], New Canal, Salisbury SP1 2AA. Telephone: 0870 505 0007. (Not lower cinemas or cinema in former café.)

YORKSHIRE
ABC [Regal], Ward's End, Halifax HX1 1BX. Telephone: 01422 352000 (infoline). (Not main foyer or lower cinemas.)
Hyde Park Picture House, Brudenell Road, Leeds LS6 1JD. Telephone: 0113 275 2045 (infoline).
Odeon, East Parade, Harrogate HG1 5LB. Telephone: 0870 505 0007. (Exterior only. Auditorium lost to subdivision.)
Odeon, Blossom Street, York YO2 2AJ. Telephone: 0870 505 0007. (Exterior, foyer and main auditorium.)

SCOTLAND
Cameo, Home Street, Tollcross, Edinburgh. Telephone: 0131 228 4141 (infoline). (Not small second screen.)
Glasgow Film Theatre, Rose Street, Glasgow G3 6RB. Telephone: 0141 332 6535. (Not small second auditorium.)
Odeon [New Victoria], Clerk Street, Edinburgh EH8 9JH. Telephone: 0870 505 0007. (Only exterior and auditorium in former balcony.)

WALES
Coliseum, Avenue Road, Portmadoc, Gwynedd LL49 9HD. Telephone: 01766 512108.

SOME IMPORTANT FORMER CINEMAS
Some buildings with important interiors that remained closed in March 2001 have been omitted.

DERBYSHIRE
Ritz, South Street, Ilkeston. (Bingo club.)

ESSEX
Mecca [Ritz], Quarry Hill, Grays. (Bingo club.)

KENT
Dreamland, Marine Terrace, Margate. (Bingo club. Cinemas in former balcony are of no interest.)

LANCASHIRE (including Manchester and Merseyside)
Apollo, Ardwick Green, Manchester. (Music venue.)
Gala [Grand], Lord Street, Southport. (Bingo club.)

LEICESTERSHIRE
Odeon, Rutland Street, Leicester. (Closed. Exterior only.)

LONDON

Academy [Astoria], Stockwell Road, Brixton, SW2. (Music venue.)
Apollo [Gaumont Palace/Odeon], Queen Caroline Street, Hammersmith, W6. (Live theatre.)
Apollo [New Victoria], Wilton Road, Victoria, SW1. (Live theatre.)
Coronet [Odeon], Parsons Hill, Woolwich, SE18. (Disused. Exterior only.)
Ealing Christian Centre [Avenue/Odeon/Coronet], Northfield Avenue, Ealing, W5. (Church.)
The Forum, Highgate Road, Kentish Town, NW5. (Music venue.)
Gala [Dominion/Granada], Acton, W3. (Bingo club.)
Gala [Granada], Mitcham Road, Tooting, SW17. (Bingo club.)
Gala [Granada], Powis Street, Woolwich, SE18. (Bingo club.)
Islamic Centre England [Picture House], 140 Maida Vale, NW6. (Community centre.)
Mecca [Regal/ABC], Camberwell Road, Camberwell, SE5. (Bingo club.)
Mecca [Carlton/ABC], Essex Road, Islington, N1. (Bingo club.)
Mecca [Gaumont State], High Street, Kilburn, NW6. (Bingo club.)
Mecca [Troxy], Commercial Road, Stepney, E1. (Bingo club.)
National Club [Grange], Kilburn High Road, NW6. (Nightclub.)
Universal Church of the Kingdom of God [Astoria/Odeon/Rainbow], Seven Sisters Road, Finsbury Park, N4. (Church.)

MIDDLESEX

Mecca [Savoy], Burnt Oak Broadway, Edgware. (Bingo club.)
Regals [Regal], High Street, Uxbridge. (Nightclub.)
Zoroastrian Centre for Europe [Grosvenor/Gaumont/Odeon], Alexandra Avenue, Rayners Lane, Harrow. (Place of worship.)

NOTTINGHAMSHIRE

Capitol, Churchfield Lane, Radford, Nottingham. (Bingo club.)

SHROPSHIRE

Gala [Granada], Castle Gates, Shrewsbury. (Bingo club.)

SOMERSET

Forum, Southgate Street, Bath. (Church and concert hall.)
Mecca [Gaumont/Odeon], Corporation Street, Taunton. (Bingo club.)

STAFFORDSHIRE

Picture House, Bridge Street, Stafford. (Pub.)
Regent, Piccadilly, Hanley. (Live theatre.)

SUFFOLK

Regent, St Helens Street, Ipswich. (Live theatre.)

SURREY

Mecca [Gaumont], Bishopsford Road, Rose Hill, Morden. (Bingo club.)

WEST MIDLANDS

Imperial, Darwell Street, Walsall. (Pub.)
Jehovah's Assembly Hall [Odeon], Castle Hill, Dudley. (Church.)
Mecca [Odeon], Skinner Street, Wolverhampton. (Bingo club.)
Mecca [Odeon], Kettlehouse Road, Kingstanding, Birmingham. (Bingo club.)
Mecca [Rink/Gaumont], Windmill Lane, Smethwick. (Bingo club.)

YORKSHIRE

Stephen Joseph Theatre [Odeon], Westborough, Scarborough. (Exterior only.)

SCOTLAND

Mecca Playhouse [Green's Playhouse], Kirk Road, Wishaw, North Lanarkshire. (Bingo club.)

WALES

Capones American Bar [Odeon], Clarence Place, Newport. (Exterior only. Nightclub.)
Palace, High Street, Conwy. (Bingo club.)
Waterstone's [Carlton], Oxford Street, Swansea. (Auditorium demolished – exterior and staircase restored.)

Regular visits to cinemas and former cinemas are arranged by the Cinema Theatre Association (further details from membership secretary: Neville C. Taylor, Flat One, 128 Gloucester Terrace, London W2 6HP).